Table of Conte

Contents

Introduction:

What is it?

Easy Gardening?

Compared to the traditional way of growing vegetables in long rows straight into the soil, Square Foot and indeed Raised Bed Gardening, certainly involves a lot less effort in order to produce significantly larger harvest. The reasons for this are simple, as this list suggests.

- The growing medium in a SFG is much lighter and easier to manage – no need for heavy digging equipment or back-breaking work to lift weeds.
- The small area involved allowing access from all sides, means that the plants are easy to maintain and keep in good health thereby producing the best crop possible.
- Combining Companion Planting methods means you have no need for chemical fertilizers or pest control methods.
- The compact nature of the SFG means that you have a larger harvest in a smaller area, for less effort.

Even though this method of gardening does not require any heavy digging or raking out of soil - does this mean that there is no effort involved at all, in order to grow fantastic healthy vegetables?

Ha ha – you wish! Joking apart however the fact is that anything worthwhile doing requires effort of some kind – it is a sort of universal law. Employing methods such as Square Foot Gardening though, ensures maximum returns on the minimal effort you have put into your gardening.

If you are truly looking for an effortless way to produce vegetables; I can tell you there is no such thing – unless a trip down to the supermarket can be included; although even that takes effort, only of a different kind!

With all that said however, it is beyond doubt that employing the SFG method does 'produce the goods' and there is something intensely satisfying in the whole process of growing your own vegetables, picking them from the plant, cooking them and presenting them at family mealtimes.

Apart from the fact that they are the healthiest vegetables you will ever consume, there is a great satisfaction in growing your own food that goes beyond mere effort and production; and indeed for many it has a definite spiritual benefit – as **George Bernard Shaw** once quoted..

"The best place to seek God is in a garden. You can dig for him there."

Back to SFG..
Square foot gardening is a concept or idea that was promoted back in the 1980's by Mel Bartholomew who coined the phrase 'Square Foot Gardening.' Since then it has gone from strength to strength, as the desire to grow vegetables free from harmful pollutants, as well as the need

to save money and the environment in the process; has gained in popularity.

It is now firmly planted in the gardener's consciousness as a way to maximise vegetable production whilst employing the minimum of spaces.

The name comes from the idea that a small frame measuring 4 foot by 4 foot, is sufficient to produce a good selection of vegetables over the growing season, that will equal the needs of a small family.

The box or frame is divided up into square foot sections as in the picture below. This equals a growing area of 16 square feet, sectioned into square foot spaces. This is an important aspect of the SFG as it is this intensive rotational method of planting that is the essence of the whole concept.

Properly planted and cared for, this small area of garden is able to produce an abundance of vegetables.

The actual construction materials of your SFG can vary widely – as will be discussed later - but traditionally is a simple framework of timber about 4-6 inches high. The depth very much depends on the crops you wish to grow, as root vegetable crops like carrots or parsnips for instance need a suitable depth of compost in order to grow adequately.

Cabbage or lettuce, zucchini or cucumber however will thrive quite well in only a few inches of good compost as they are of course above-ground vegetables, and so do not require depth in order to grow adequately.

Each of the foot-square spaces is occupied by a variety of vegetables, with the larger plants like potatoes and tomato for instance occupying a square all to themselves; while beets can be grown 9 to a square and carrots can be grown 16 to each square as in the example chart below.

South Facing

RADISH (16)	RADISH (16)	BEET (9)	BEET (9)
CARROTS (16)	CARROTS (16)	CUCUMBER (2)	CUCUMBER (2)
PEPPER (1)	PEPPER (1)	POTATO (1)	POTATO (1)
CORN (3)	CORN (3)	PEAS (8)	PEAS (8)

The diagram above is just an example of the way you may lay out a SFG, with the taller plants to the rear where they will not block the sunlight to the lower vegetables. The number alongside the individual plants, is the number of plants that you can grow in each individual square.

Types of plants and the numbers that can be grown in each square will be discussed in further chapters.

Why Square Foot Gardening?

Along with a growing awareness that the human race must start taking more responsibility for its environment, some people have also come to the realization that doing so actually means a win-win situation for us all in many different ways. Why is this? In a nutshell it is simply down to the fact that if we treat our environment with respect, then in turn we are rewarded with better health, both physical and mental, as well as better living conditions free of pollution where we can truly enjoy what nature has provided.

Gardening in small spaces using the Square Foot Gardening method first pioneered by Mel Bartholomew in the 1980's, is one way where individuals can start to take back control from the mega-stores with regard to food production. It enables us to grow fruit and vegetables without the need for chemical fertilizers and other pollutants that contaminate the supermarket shelves, and instead allows us to grow our produce and feed our families without at the same time damaging our surroundings, our health and our wealth!

Another big factor that promotes the Square Foot Gardening method, is simply down to the fact that it enables people with very limited space to grow their own fresh vegetables. Even individuals living in city apartments are now finding that the roof space can be ideal for SFG (along with the relevant permissions of course!), and whole communities have joined with their local authorities to release waste land for SFG projects.

Along with these already mentioned, the advantages of using this system can be summed up in the following short list.

Square Foot Advantages:

Chemical Free:

Because of the nature of this intensive gardening system, there is little or no chemicals involved either with the fertilization methods, or the pest control methods employed. Both are organic in nature and the planting rotation is done in such a way as to avoid the use of artificial stimulants or chemical sprays.

Companion planting methods are employed to a large extent in a Square Foot Garden, to ensure that each plant gets the 'best of all worlds' when it comes to growing conditions. This means that plants are grown together for mutual benefit, to control pests and to ensure proper nutrition and excellent quality produce free of chemical contamination.

Convenient:

As mentioned earlier, this method requires such a small space (4 foot x 4 foot) that it opens up the possibilities for almost anyone to consider growing their own veg. Even if you live in a city apartment and do not have any garden ground, there is the possibility to erect a SFG on the roof perhaps, or maybe even to join with a local authority gardening scheme – or create one if it does not already exist!

People who have busy work schedules can also find this way convenient in that it is much easier and less time consuming than traditional gardening methods. Weeding is reduced to a minimum as you are not using soil contaminated by weed seeds, and even when they finally raise their heads they are easily pulled out because the growing medium is not packed hard by footsteps.

Economical:

Especially relevant for those already involved in growing their own vegetables – a SFG system means that you are no longer growing heaps of veggies that end up in the compost heap because you cannot consume them fast enough! This is often the lamentable situation with regards to conventional gardening, where rows of vegetables are grown all at once; leading to wastage and a lot of hard work for nothing.

Included in this "wastage" must be not only be the expense of the seedlings or seeds, but also the cost involved in compost, fertilizer, pest control, weeding and maintenance – whether organic in nature or not.

With SFG, the vegetables are grown in an intensive yet rotational manner which is aimed at providing a **reasonable amount** of the 'green stuff ' right at the time when you can appreciate it most and put it to best use. This avoids needless waste – though it does mean that the compost heap may grow hungry!

This also means that this method is more cost effective than traditional growing, as you are not bearing the financial cost of producing vegetables to end up in the compost heap!

Good For You!

Yes, I know that this might be stating the obvious – however the fact is that growing your own vegetables in such an easy laid-back way, is not only good for you with regards to your general nutritional intake; but gardening in general is known to be great therapy! Coupled with the fact that it is physically easier to maintain a SFG (no more digging heavy water-logged soil involving back-breaking labour), it means more time to relax and enjoy your produce.

In fact I should have maybe laboured this point under the 'Economical' section as growing vegetables as well as caring for livestock or pets, are recognized as being excellent for reducing the sessions at the therapist for stress related problems – and we know how expensive they can be!

Outline Of Main Points (As Taken from my <u>Square Foot Vs Raised Bed Gardening</u> Book)

The Main Benefits of A SFG

- **Size:** With the growing bed area being so small, it means that this technique can be used even by city dwellers, as long as they have a tiny area to place their SFG.
- **Variety**: Rotational planting method means that you can have a good mixture of different veggies throughout the growing season.

- **Easy Maintained**: Easy to keep and maintain once the plants are established. Loose compost means no hard work involved in weeding for instance.
- **Natural Pest Control:** The application of companion planting, as well as the mixture of vegetable types, means that pest control can be accomplished without the need for chemical pesticides
- **No Chemical Fertilizer**: Again, this is accomplished by using Companion Planting methods, along with crop rotation, and a good quality compost mixture.
- **Longer Growing Season**: Since the growing medium is raised slightly from the ground, and has ideal conditions for growing; the actual growing season is extended beyond that of a conventional garden.
- **Portable:** Especially with regard to the shallow bed model, this type of garden can be lifted and transported to a suitable location – provided it has a base of course!

Conclusion:

Ok, well so much for the benefits of the SFG method of growing vegetables; I hope that if you had any doubts about it before now, you are on your way to gaining an understanding of just what the fuss is all about regarding Square Foot Gardening; now for the practical application of growing vegetables using this process.

NOTES/MY TO-DO PAGE

Constructing Your SFG

Basic Model SFG:

The basic construction model for your SFG is simplicity itself, and involves making a four-sided frame, mainly from timber, and open top and bottom. However that is just the start of the story – as they say, and different adaptations on this theme can be used depending on circumstances such as whether or not you want a portable SFG; or indeed what types of plants you wish to grow.

The construction materials themselves, apart from timber, can also include bricks, cinder blocks, straw bales, or just about anything that you can make a barrier with to hold in the compost. With that in mind here are a couple of examples of the timber materials that you will need according to the model you choose.

Traditional SFG:

To construct a basic SFG, you will need the following (untreated) timber materials; Cedar or Oak is best, however redwood will still last for approx 10 years or so. It is best to use untreated timber to prevent contaminants from the treatment leaching into your composting material – and from there to the plants themselves.

- 2 lengths of 6 inches x 1.5" x 4 foot
- 2 lengths 6 inches x 1.5" x 4 foot 3 inches
- 4 short posts 3 x 3 x 12"
- Galvanised nails or screw-nails to secure timber to posts.

- 6 lengths thin strapping or roll of baling twine to mark out the boxes.
- 16 - 3" screws
- Short screws or nails for strapping (optional)

Tools Needed for the job..
- Crosscut saw
- Small Club Hammer
- Electric drill or cordless screwdriver
- 1/8th drill bit
- Measuring tape.

Basic layout of your SFG

Diagram 1

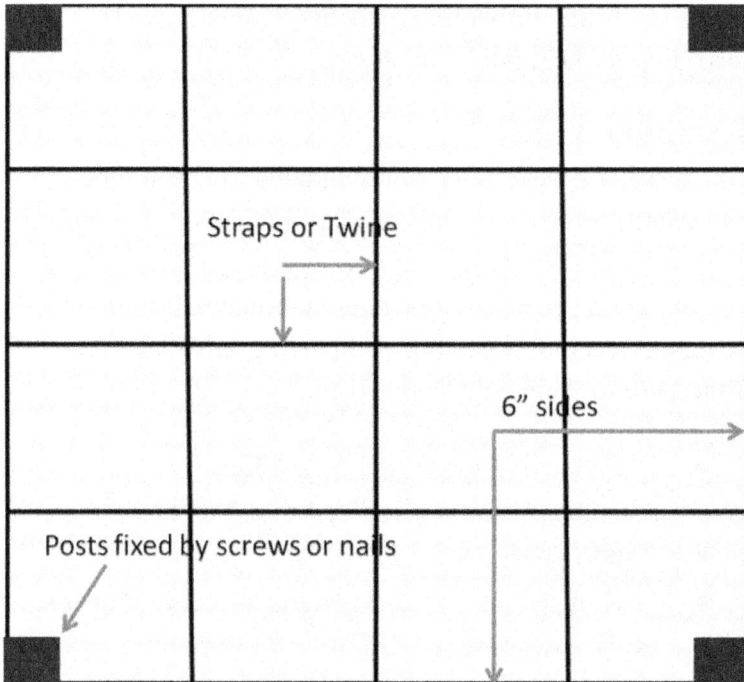

View from the side…

Diagram 2

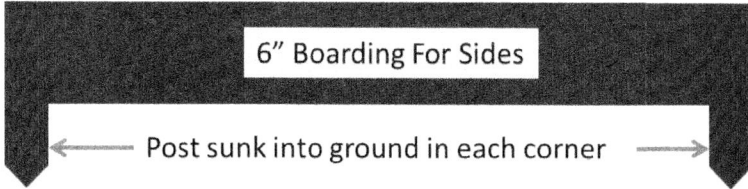

6" Boarding For Sides

Post sunk into ground in each corner

Constructing the frame itself can be done in two ways, depending on whether your 'box' is fixed to the ground or is a portable version. The portable version is exactly the same except the posts will be the same depth as the sides (4" is advisable as any deeper will make it unmanageable) , and it will have a base made from ½ inch plywood in order to hold the compost.

Traditional assembly:
First clear and level the area of ground that you intend to use for your SFG. This should be North-South facing and have at least 7 hours direct sunshine per day, though 8 or more is best. Be sure to avoid the shade of large trees, shrubs, and buildings when selecting a spot for your SFG.

Next cut your timber to the required lengths. Next lay out the two **shorter lengths** that will make up the sides and after drilling two pilot holes at each end with the 1/8th bit, attach the posts using the cordless screwdriver and screws as per diagram 2. When this is done present the two longer sections to the frame and fix according to the diagram below.

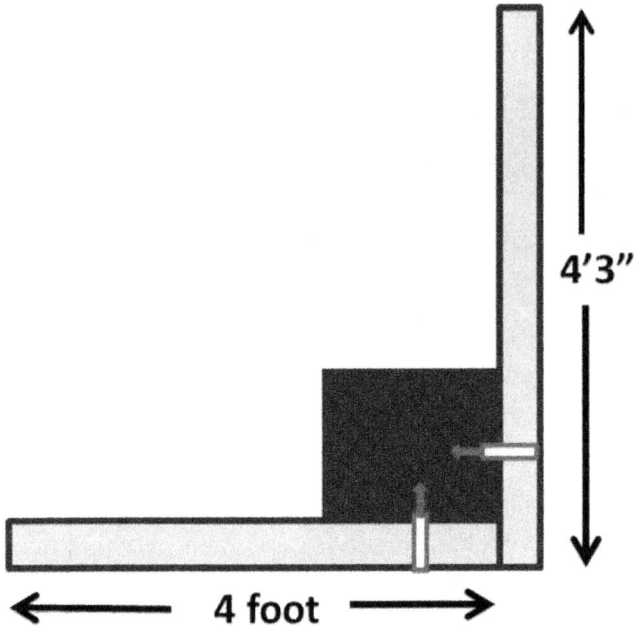

4'3"

4 foot

By using this method of construction you are making up for the thickness of the timbers and are left with a square with **the inside measurement** of 4 foot by 4 foot exactly, if constructed with 1.5 inch timbers.

This frame should then be placed into position and each corner post gently tapped down into the ground with the Club hammer an inch or two at a time for each post, until the sides sit on the ground surface.

Alternatively the frame can be assembled piece at a time in-situ, though I usually find this a bit more awkward.

With your frame in position, it is a simple matter to measure out your frame into square foot boxes as per diagram 1, and either fix in place your strapping material, or knock a nail into the wood at the proper points and twist garden twine to form the boxes.

Portable Assembly:

This is basically the same as the traditional, but the corner posts are the same depth as the sides, as they do not require to be fixed to the ground.

Additionally you will have to supply a 4 foot square piece of ½" to ¾" plywood for the base.

When the frame is assembled, simply lay it on a flat surface and fix the plywood to form the base. Fix the ply into position using rust-resistant screw nails preferably.

When this is done then drill half a dozen or so holes in the base for drainage.

I would only recommend a portable SFG that is no more than 4 inches deep, as any deeper will make it heavy to move around; even so this is a task that will require two people.

With this in mind then it is obvious that a portable SFG is not suitable for root vegetables, but is perfectly suitable for most beets or brassica.

Other SFG Constructions:

As mentioned, Square Foot Gardens can be constructed using a variety of different materials; all that you are attempting to do is form a small area 4 foot square that will hold compost. I would advise however that you do not use heavily treated timber, as much as this would make sense in normal conditions when assembling wood in an outside environment; to do so in the vicinity of vegetables risks contamination that may kill the plant altogether or simply contaminate them (and yourself) with chemicals.

Either way it is not a good result! Far better to allow for the fact that your untreated timber will 'only' last 10 years or so before it has to be replaced. Either that or consider artificial decking material that never rots and will last you a life-time.

One construction material that I quite like – though it may not be aesthetically pleasing for everyone – is the hollow cinder block SFG example that I have included at the beginning of this book. The reason for this is that the hollow blocks can be filled with compost and planted with either micro-crops (onion, scallion, herbs etc) or used to plant French Marigold for instance following the companion planting method – **more on this in the following chapters**.

SFG Accessories

One of the exciting aspects of the SFG – as indeed with the Raised Bed Garden – is the ability to easily change it to suite your own particular gardening requirements; this is particularly the case when considering weather or discouraging the pests (in all their varieties) that may come to visit!

In the picture below you will see an example of a mini-greenhouse effect that utilises two traditional SFG's to form a longer growing area.

The frame is simply constructed from plastic 1" piping that you can obtain from most DIY stores or plumbing suppliers. This is attached to the inside of the frame using method in the picture underneath. Access to the inside is achieved by simply to lifting up the polythene sides –

which are in turn fixed between two lengths of 2" x 1" timber.

Once lifted they can easily be held up by fixing a couple of 'S'shaped holding brackets to the frame; thereby allowing you to service your SFG.

If you are in a particularly exposed windy area then it may be necessary to fix the 2 x 1 strap to the SFG frame when closed - or better still to strong fixings in the ground.

The end piece of polythene covering is simply held together with a couple of suitable crocodile clips from the DIY store.

This same method can also be used to attach a bird-proof nylon mesh that will protect your strawberries and other fruits, as well as lettuce and young plants from the predations of Blackbirds and Pigeons.

If you have used the hollow cinder block method to construct your SFG, then simply sink the pipework into the hollows in the blocks to achieve the same result.

SFG Raised Bed:

Square foot Gardening is similar in many ways to Raised Bed Gardening, in fact it could be argued that they are both versions of the same concept inasmuch as they are both 'raised' to some extent or other. If you would like to know more about the two concepts 'side by side' as it were, then please check out my book on the subject '**Square Foot Gardening Vs Raised Bed Gardening.**'

Without going into the all different workings of the two systems however, suffice it to say that many of the methods for growing vegetables is exactly the same; and the particular aspect of the Raised Bed method – the fact that it is traditionally raised to 18-24 inches high – is something that the SF gardener can also utilize to great advantage.

By raising the sides to a higher level, it means that not only is it more convenient to service the plot as there is not so much bending over; but it is also easier to keep insect and vermin free.

One simple method for keeping Carrot fly at bay for instance is to make sure you surround your bed with a small screen (fleece will do) about 24 inches from the ground, as the carrot fly does not fly above this height as a general rule. Depending on the height of your Raised Bed then this might only involve a screen 6" high – easily attached to the side of your Bed.

As for the construction itself, simply calculate the materials to suit your desired height. For instance a 4 x 4 SFG at 18" high instead of the example at 6" will need in the way of materials..

- 6 lengths of 6 inches x 1.5" x 4 foot
- 6 lengths 6 inches x 1.5" x 4 foot 3 inches
- 4 short posts 3 x 3 x 24"
- Galvanised nails or screw-nails to secure timber to posts.

- 6 lengths thin strapping or roll of baling twine to mark out the boxes.

There is of course a downside to a deeper bed – more materials not only in the construction, but also more compost needed to fill it. However I would add that if you just intend to plant vegetables such as brassicas, beets etc that do not require deep soil; then all you need do is be sure that you have a bout 6-8 inches of good compost on the surface, and fill the rest with any bricks or rubble that you can get for free – thereby saving money on expensive composting material.

Multiple SFG's

At the risk of stating the obvious…I have to emphasise that you can have more than one SFG !

This is especially the case if you wish to grow a bigger range of crops, or more of one particular crop, or indeed if you just have more mouths to feed – perhaps this is a community project?

Whatever your reason for desiring more than 1 SFG, there are couple of important aspects that you must bear in mind.

First you must ensure that they all get the maximum benefit from the hours of sunshine or shade depending on what exactly you are growing.

Secondly – and something that is often overlooked until it is too late – Spacing!

Make sure that you have enough space between the boxes to push a wheelbarrow, and if it is for the physically disadvantaged make sure that a wheelchair can freely manoeuvre your SFG's.

Usually a minimum gap of 24-30 inches is adequate for most needs, but up to 3 foot is required for wheelchair access.

It hardly needs illustrated, but just in case; here is an example of a typical SFG layout for multiple installations.

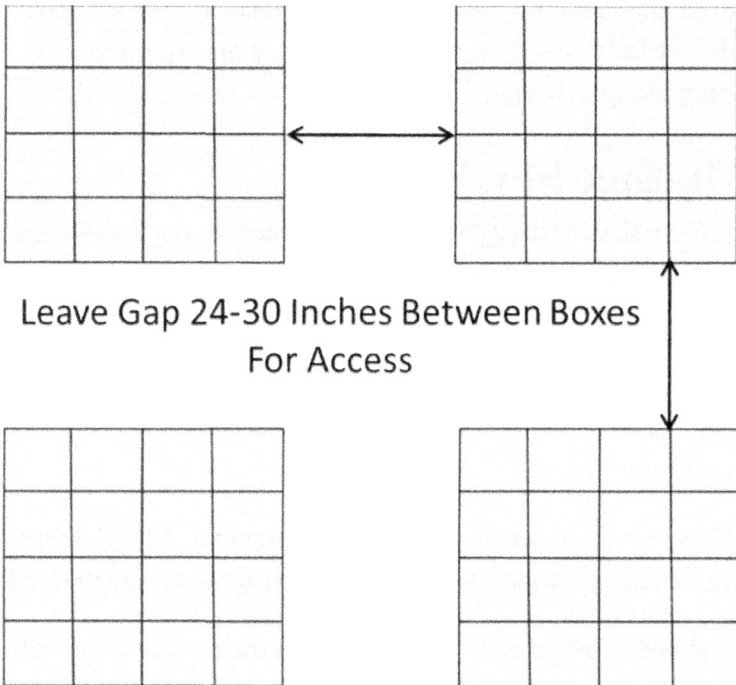

Leave Gap 24-30 Inches Between Boxes
For Access

Not To Scale

NOTES/MY TO-DO PAGE

Infilling Your SFG

SFG Infill Mixes:

The correct composting material is essential if you want to get the best results out of your SFG, this is particularly the case if you want to restrict the use of chemical fertilizers in your growing practices.

Of course the Mel Bartholomew recipe for SFG is well known – 1/3 Vermiculite, 1/3 Peat moss, 1/3 compost – and has proven itself to be very effective. However don't let this put you off mixing your own 'magic mix' for your SFG.

For instance Vermiculite helps keep soil light, allows for good airflow, and absorbs and retains water – thus it makes a great addition to any SFG mix. However this can be quite expensive if you have more than one SFG planned and I have substituted this with the cheaper Perlite, with no ill effects that I could notice. I would also add that provided you have a good mix of organic material in your compost, it is possible to either of the two and still have healthy crops.

Likewise many folks of a more environmental persuasion are uncomfortable with using Peat Moss in their mix as this is in their mind just another attack on the eco-system as Peat Moss is a non-sustainable product that takes centuries to develop and its extraction irretrievably harms the environment by releasing greenhouse gases into the air.

So is it absolutely essential to use Peat Moss in your SFG? The short answer is no it is not, and it is possible to substitute peat moss with more sustainable products such as coconut coir dust which helps soil absorb and retain moisture in much the same way that peat does.

This product is produced from the waste product of the coconut plant – the hairy husk or outer coating of the nut itself – making it a sustainable alternative to peat moss.

Will Vegetables grow in a pure compost mix?
Short answer – Absolutely! As an example check out the pic below and you will see a prize Zucchini growing on top of a composting bin – pure compost no 'magic mix' involved.

Generally though, unless your compost has been through a riddle to sort out the rough from the smooth; the 'pure' compost can be a little untidy and unmanageable for some veggies that grow better in a more compact (not compressed) growing medium.

It is also true that good compost is usually at a premium as it takes some time to develop, and so the other additions also help maximize your distribution capabilities as well as ventilation and drainage – both essential ingredients for the successful vegetable garden.

The pure compost may also be a little strong depending on what its makeup has been, and so adding other material has the effect of diluting the mix.

Zucchini growing in compost bin

Try Something Different!

When it comes down to it, gardening in some ways is not unlike cooking – yes there are certain rules that must be followed but if you do not have all the ingredients for a particular recipe, then try something else! You just never know if you might come across your own 'Mel's Mix' of compost that will do the job perfectly fine.

One rule however that is most important when infilling your SFG or indeed Raised Bed, is **never to use just soil**. Even if it is the best quality topsoil it will compress over time and make it difficult to maintain, as well as difficult for the plants to grow in.

A good SFG mix has to be light and airy, this will promote excellent growth and be easy to maintain with regard to weed-pulling and other general gardening tasks.

Apart from the mixes already mentioned, here are some mixes for my SFG and Raised Beds that I have had great success with.

Mix 1: 60% compost, 20% washed sand, 20% peat moss.

Mix 2: 40% compost, 20% fish meal, 30% coconut coir and 10% good topsoil.

Mix 3: 50% compost, 20% vermiculite (or perlite), 30% peat moss.

Mix 4: 50% compost, 30% peat moss, 20% quality topsoil.

Mix 5: 40% compost, 40% peat moss, 20% vermiculite.

Bottom Line - Give the plants what they want with regard to light, nutrients, water , air and temperature – and they will delight you by producing excellent vegetables.

Volumes:
The actual volume of material required of course depends on the depth of the SFG, however this is a simple calculation. Every 6 inches in depth for your 4 x 4 SFG requires 8 cubic feet of mix.

About Compost:

In a nutshell, compost is the term used for organic matter that has been decomposed (rotted) and recycled as a soil conditioner, to improve crop growth performance.

This is something that you must think about long before you need the compost, in most cases a year at least. Your SFG needs compost that is well rotted and crumbly to the feel. If it is still smelly then it is not ready for the garden yet.

The process of making your own compost is simple enough, as it is basically a load of organic material such as vegetable trimmings, grass cuttings, fallen leaves etc, that are dumped into a bin or wooden framework and left to decompose in a process that can take months or even years. That's the simple answer; however there are certain things that you **should not add** to a compost heap such as..

- **Inorganic material:** Plastic and polythene will not break down to form compost. Obvious I know, but it had to be said!
- **Pet Poop:** Never add dog or cat droppings to the compost heap, as this can add several disease organisms that can turn your compost toxic.
- **Fish, fats, meat, bones and dairy**: These should not be added as they can just attract vermin, and cause your compost to smell badly.
- **Coal ash**: timber ash is fine for compost as it adds valuable potash, but coal ash is not as it can add high levels of sulphur to your compost.

- **Coloured paper**: Coloured paper can contain heavy metals and other toxic materials. These should not be added to your compost.
- **Diseased plants**: Any diseased or infested plants that you have to lift up should be burned or otherwise disposed of. Do not add to the compost as they will most likely end up back in your garden to repeat the cycle all over again!

Compost Mixes:

There are many different mixes of compost that will suit certain plants more than others, and this is great if you are specializing in a specific area like growing giant pumpkins! However if you have a source of well-rotted manure, then this is ideal for crops such as tomatoes, beans, peas, leeks - in fact just about anything, as rotted manure is a great source of nitrogen which every plant needs in different quantities.

There are certain plants that also make valuable additions to the compost heap such as nettles, which speed up decomposition and add valuable nitrogen, or comfrey, which is a terrific source of potash (potassium) and has a high carbon to nitrogen ratio – which is ideal for most plants and perfect for tomatoes, fruit and berries.

If you are working a homestead or hobby farm then you almost certainly have access to chicken manure! This is very rich in nitrogen and a fantastic addition to your compost. Be sure though to let it rot for at least 1 year to kill off any parasites or eggs that may be in it; also it needs this time to 'mellow' otherwise it is too strong in nitrogen for most plants to tolerate.

When using manure of any kind you have the option to add it to your composting heap while they are both still in the process of decomposing; or you may add the fully decomposed manure directly to your SFG as part of the mix.

When has manure decomposed enough to use?
You will know when the manure has finished decomposing when it has a deep 'earthy' smell – not smelling of dung; and the material itself should be relatively dry and crumbly when handled.

If it still smells of dung then it has not finished decomposing and should be left for a further few weeks or even months.

Here is a chart to show just what the different animal dungs 'bring to the table' with regard to percentage values of nutrients.

	NITROGEN	PHOSPHORUS	POTASH
Average farmyard manure	0.64	0.23	0.32
Pure pig dung	0.48	0.58	0.36
Pure cow dung	0.44	0.29	0.49

Horse Manure	0.49	0.29	0.58
Deep litter on straw	0.80	0.55	0.48
Fresh Poultry Dung	1.66	0.91	0.45
Pigeon Dung	5.84	2.10	1.77

As you may notice from this chart – it would pay to keep in with your local pigeon fancier – or keep some birds yourself!

Making Good Compost

If you pile up vegetable matter and let it rot over a period of time, then you will get compost. However if you want to make good compost over a shorter time then there are certain steps you have to follow.

Compost is basically formed when vegetable or organic matter is broken down by aerobic organisms. These are fungi and bacteria, which need oxygen to live. In order for the bacteria to break down the cellulose in plant matter they need nitrogen, and the more nitrogen they get the quicker they will do their job and the quicker you can achieve good compost.

Typical Compost Bin Layout

Top Layer - Leaves

Wet Greens

Dry Leaves

Water Well

Manure or Soil

Wet Greens

Dry Leaves

Water Well

Manure or Soil

Wet Greens

Dry Leaves

Branches or Pallet

Compost Ingredients:

- **Carbon** (Dried Matter)**:** Dried leaves, straw, wood chips, grass, small twigs.
- **Nitrogen** (fresh matter): Vegetable scraps, lawn clippings, weeds, manure.
- **Soil:** The addition of good soil adds minerals and micro-organisms to the compost, thereby stimulating aerobic composition

This layering process – including watering well between layers - generates significant heat which also kills disease organisms and weed seeds etc, in effect making it suitable for use in the garden. If there is a shortage of nitrogen then the whole process is lengthened. The job of the good compost maker is to see that this is not the case and provide suitable quantities of air, moisture and nitrogen to the mix.

With all this in mind a good composter should be constructed in such a way as to ensure good ventilation to the mix; as well as allow for turning the compost (for aeration).

Traditionally Nitrogen can be added to the mix by adding fresh dung as the nitrogen is in the urine; or by adding suitable plants such as nettles (without the roots) and grass clippings which are rich in nitrogen.

As different materials decay at different times, it is also advisable to have not just one composter, but three at least if you have the space for them. This way you can really take control over your composting efforts.

Here is a good example of home-made compost bins from pallets acquired from the local DIY store for free. The fronts of the bins are set in place in such a way that they can easily be removed for turning the compost.

Although this model will work just fine as it allows the air to circulate well; the addition of 1" chicken mesh stapled to the sides will help to keep in the compost as well as keep out unwanted vermin. With this in mind you may also want to consider a cover for your bins – though remember to water periodically to stop the compost drying out completely.

Every-Day Composting:

Whilst composting is generally carried out in a process involving turning and compost rotation, there is also what I like to call 'Every-day' compost.

This is composting in its simplest form, designed with the householder in mind who has to keep it basic and simply wants to recycle their organic waste products such as kitchen vegetable waste, as and when they have them available.

Modern composting bins like the one below are ok but are not designed to be turned over; indeed to do so would add the new material to the old and mess up the composting process. This design therefore is intended to make a little compost at a time and the rotted material to be removed from the bottom of the bin via the access panel provided.

The fact that the dark green plastic warms up quickly helps speed up the composting process.

Composters can be made from many kinds of material, the main thing being that they allow the circulation of air and easy access for maintenance.

Positioning Compost Bins:
As for the siting of the composters themselves; the obvious answer is do not use up valuable growing space if you can

avoid it. As long as your composter gets enough sunshine to warm it up slightly but not dry it out, then this will do perfectly well. Keep the bins at least 6 feet away from overhanging trees, and position where they get adequate light and a free flow of air.

How Long?

As for how long you will have to wait before you get great compost for your efforts, I'm afraid there is no definite answer! This is because of several factors that will influence the time it takes for the material to break down.

- The actual material itself – grass cuttings break down faster than fallen leaves for instance which can certainly take over 1 year and need a fair amount of turning.
- The amount of nitrogen in the mix. Low nitrogen-rich plants or lack of manure will slow down the process.
- Ventilation. A well ventilated composter will work much faster than one that does not allow for an adequate flow of air.
- Turning your compost regularly will increase the composting process.
- Moisture content is also very important in speeding up the process. The compost should be damp like a wrung-out cloth in order to operate properly.

With all that said; in general terms rough mulching compost, ideal for setting around shrubs and bushes, or putting in the bottom of a planting hole, can usually be achieved in 3-4 months.

A smoother compost, for adding to your SFG or growing seedlings for instance, will usually take no less than 6 months to achieve – usually much longer. If conditions are not ideal then composting can take several years to achieve; making it worth that little bit extra effort to speed up the process!

Composting Materials Time-line:
Here is a short list of composting materials and the time taken to compost in ideal conditions.

Materials taking 6 months +
Kitchen vegetable trimmings (beware - stems and stalks take 2-3 years or more), annual weeds, fruit peel, lawn trimmings (no more than 15cm thick).

Material taking 1 – 2 years
Hedge clippings and prunings (except conifers and evergreens which will take more than 3 years to break down completely), paper and cardboard, autumn leaves.

Material taking 3 years +
Thick stalks and stems of plants, evergreens including holly or conifers, eggshells, sawdust & wood shavings, or thick layers of grass clippings.
Any other organic material that is large and bulky will naturally take longer to compost.

Another Option?

Finally, if you have no space to compost, or no time or whatever – consider your local authority! Many municipal authorities are composting as part of their environmental efforts, this is highly regulated and usually excellent quality – and it is often given away free or for very little cost!

If that option is not available or you would like to get started growing your vegetables immediately; then you can certainly go for store-bought compost – maybe even Mel's Mix itself, while your own composting efforts are a 'work in progress.'

Making Organic 'Tea'

When using the SFG method in particular and following the composting and Companion planting methods included here, there should be no need at all for chemical fertilizers. The SFG method of organic growing means that your growing medium (your soil) is forever replenishing itself, and the most it should need is a 'top-up' of compost or 'green tea' at the peak of the growing season.

Where possible use rain water, or even water from a river or pond to make your 'tea.'

What is Green Tea?

This is simply a phrase coined for a liquid solution made by adding water to organic matter and letting it 'brew' into a nutrient rich feed for your plants. There are any number of recipes for this concoction, but here are 4 common recipes you may wish to consider.

- **Compost Tea**: Place <u>mature</u> compost into a large drum, filling about half way. Fill to the top with water. Stir thoroughly then let this mix brew for a period of 5 days or so, then strain of the compost and add the liquid to the base of the plants.
- **Horse Manure Tea:** Follow the recipe for the compost tea, but add only 1/3rd manure and two thirds water. I have found this feed particularly effective for Tomatoes.
- **Comfrey Tea:** Rich in potash and nitrogen, Comfrey is worth growing in any patch of ground for this ability alone. Add a large bunch of chopped-up comfrey to your water bin, place a brick on top and fill with water. Let it brew for about two weeks before adding to your veggies.
- **Nettle Tea:** This tea does not contain much in the way of phosphates, but has usable amounts of nitrogen, iron, and magnesium. After donning heavy gloves to avoid the stinging nettles! Choose young plants without seeds or roots and put a large clump into a pail. Chop up with sheers and ¾ fill the pail with water . Stir thoroughly and leave to mature for 5-10 days.

General Guidelines:

Be aware that E coli and other harmful bacteria can be present in any manure and so must be handled with due care. Do not feed compost or manure tea to plants where the edible part lies on the ground – i.e. strawberries, cucumber, marrow etc. And stop using 3 weeks before vegetables are to be harvested.

Organic tea is usually applied once daily when the fruits have started to appear.

Always wash your hands thoroughly after using manure products of any kind – particularly before eating!

For just a little extra effort you can grow good healthy crops without polluting the environment and your body, by using good healthy compost.

Chemical fertilizers do not feed the land, instead they give the plants themselves a quick boost of nitrogen and phosphates, leaving the land barren and useless for future generations. Just like an addictive drug, these chemicals have to be applied on an annual basis in order to gain any benefit at all for the plants; each year the dose has to be increased in order to get the same results.

This is known as the 'law of diminishing returns' and is the exact opposite of what you will achieve by following the old ways of composting properly and diverse rotational growing.

When applying compost to the soil you are in effect feeding the land, and the land in return will bless you and future generations with healthy crops for years, even centuries to come.

NOTES/MY TO-DO PAGE

NB. NO BRASICAS — DON'T WORK
IN THE SOIL.

PEAS,
BEANS,
BEETS
SPRING ONION
CARROT
TURNIPS

Planting Out Your SFG

South Facing

BASIL (4)	BEET (9)	BEET (9)	LAVENDER (1)
RADISH (16)	ONIONS (4)	ONIONS (4)	RADISH (16)
CHIVES (16)	CARROTS (16)	CARROTS (16)	CHIVES (16)
BEANS (8)	BEANS (8)	PEAS (8)	PEAS (8)

The above diagram is just one planting pattern for use with the SFG concept, although it should be noted that as companion plants, growing tomatoes near potatoes is not ideal as they are both in the same 'family' and so are prone to blight and use up the same nutrients from the soil.

At the rear of the area you will have your tallest plants, like tomato or corn, so that they do not block precious sunlight from the other plants. As the planting progresses to the front south facing area, then the general idea is to plant in such a way as to give every plant the amount of exposure to the sun that it needs to reach optimum growth.

Likewise if you are growing climbers like peas or beans, you would erect a simple frame or trellis work to the rear for them to climb up.

Seeds or Seedlings?

When it comes time to plant out your SFG (having first of all decided on the plants you wish to grow) you then have to decide whether or not you will start with seeds or seedlings.

I will not spend a lot of time on this issue as it very much depends on your individual circumstances or indeed inclination! Suffice it to say that planting seeds – especially in an SFG – is cheaper, but for many not as reliable as planting established seedlings which will give you an instant veggie garden. You can grow the seedlings yourself and bring them on in a greenhouse or other heated facility, or indeed purchase them from your local garden center.

If you are planting directly into your SFG from seed however, this is perfectly acceptable and as mentioned it is certainly cheaper as you are not setting out long rows of seeds – most of which are wasted when it comes time to thin them out. Do bear in mind however that planting directly into your SFG usually means a delay until the weather is warm enough. This in turn will mean that you have a shorter growing season in which to benefit from your efforts.

This can be countered to some extend by planting them under a polythene mini-greenhouse as in the earlier pictures, or even a covering of gardeners fleece if it is not too cold. Because of the dense nature of the SFG method only a few seeds more than the actual plants you require have to be planted, meaning that there is less to thin out when they eventually peek through the soil.

Check the back of the seed packet to find the ideal germination conditions, as well as the instructions for planting.

Instructions for growing a number of popular vegetables will be included in later chapters.

Veggie Matters

Importance of Diversity:

Diversity and crop rotation lie at the very heart of the SFG. The very opposite of the mono-culture principles of commercial growing, which concentrates one crop in the same place year after year and has to throw chemicals and pesticides at it in order to achieve significant growth; growing in small spaces gains its strength and growing success from the range of different plants grown in a small space and rotated on a regular basis.

Apart from the excellent infill material that you are now about to plant your vegetables in; the main points to consider when planning your SFG, and the things that will assure you of success are down to these two main points.

1: Crop Diversity

By organising the plants in a confined space like the SFG, and planting a number of different vegetables; it means that you are not so prone to attack by insect or disease. This is the problem that most conventional gardeners face – as well as the commercial organisations. Different crops attract the predations of common species of insects or disease, making a diverse mixture of plants less prone to an all-out attack.

This is also the backbone and the principle behind a concept called 'Companion Planting' where crops are planted alongside other crops or even flowers that will be of mutual benefit in helping control pests as well as encourage growth. There will be more on Companion Planting in later chapters.

2: Crop Rotation

For centuries farmers have understood the importance of crop rotation, and indeed it was the back-bone of farming up until recent times, and the growth of chemical fertilizers.

However by utilizing the principle of crop rotation in our SFG, we can be assured that the plants that are grown on previously occupied space will most benefit from the nutrients that the previous incumbents have left behind. Remember the principle behind organic growing is that you are feeding the land and not just giving the veggies a 'quick shot in the arm.'

Choosing Your Veggies:

To help you choose which vegetables you would like to grow, there are several factors you have to take into account.

- **Your climate:** Don't try and grow plants in a climate not suited to them. For instance tender plants can be very vulnerable to frosts, but hardier vegetables can cope with bouts of cooler weather. Sometimes you can help things along though by covering your SFG with a mini-greenhouse type frame.
- **Growing Season:** Consider the length of your growing season in comparison to the length of time to mature your crop.
- **What do you like?** Don't grow what you cannot eat if possible – obvious I know but sometimes you can be tempted just by the challenge of growing something different – this usually just leads to a lot of waste though!
- **Soil Quality:** This of course should not be a problem if you have followed the general guide for infilling your SFG ☺

Next we have to consider the types of vegetables and what order we can plant them in to get the best results. Here is a list of the most common vegetables along with the numbers that can be grown in each foot-square block.

Plants	Approx Days to Harvest	No Per Square
ASPARAGUS (after shoots appear)	14-21	1
BASIL	40-45	4
BROCCOLI	85-110	1
BEETS	50-70	9
BEANS (pole)	70-80	4-8
BRUSSELS SPROUTS	85-100	1
CABBAGE	90-100	1
CAULIFLOWER	85-110	1
CARROT	70	16
CELERY	60-65	9
CORN	80	3
CHIVES	80	16
CUCUMBER	55	2
DILL	65-70	1
EGGPLANT (Aubergine)	110-120	1
GARLIC	90-100	4
LETTUCE	40-80	4
LEEK	100-125	9
MINT	30-45	1
ONIONS	95-110	4
OREGANO	50-60	1
PARSELY	80-90	4
PEAS	70-80	8
PEPPERS	70-80	1
POTATO	80-100	1
RADISH	28	16
ROSEMARY	85	1
SAGE	60-90	1
STRAWBERRY	60-90	4
SCALLION (Spring Onion)	60-70	16

SPINACH	45-50	9
SQUASH	85-90	1
TOMATOES	70-75	1
WATER MELON	80-85	1
ZUCCHINI (courgette)	80	1

Another important aspect of growing plants in such a confined space is the fact that some plants grow well together and some do not. As well as this, some plants benefit from growing in the same space that's others have just vacated (been harvested), owing to the nutrition that they have left in the soil behind them.

South Facing

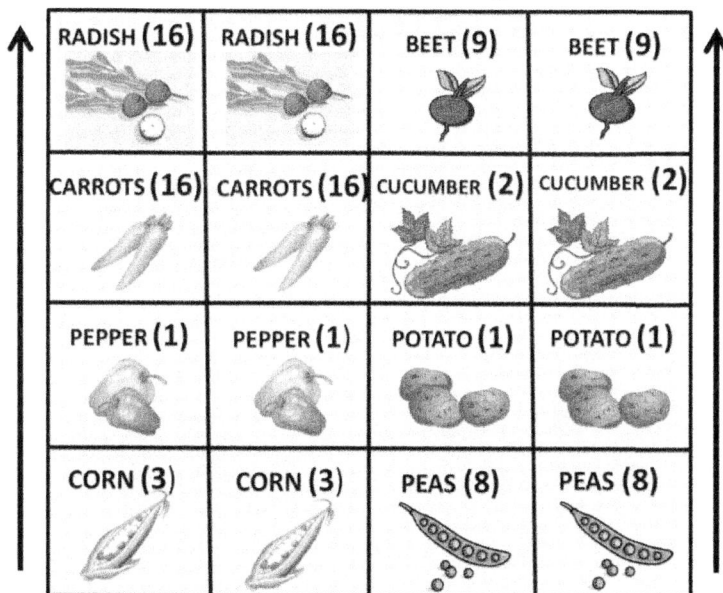

RADISH (16)	RADISH (16)	BEET (9)	BEET (9)
CARROTS (16)	CARROTS (16)	CUCUMBER (2)	CUCUMBER (2)
PEPPER (1)	PEPPER (1)	POTATO (1)	POTATO (1)
CORN (3)	CORN (3)	PEAS (8)	PEAS (8)

Large leafy plants such as Zucchini, Aubergine, Water melon etc that also have large fruits; will normally take **two**

squares to the one plant in order to grow to their full potential.

Planting vegetables in this way is an important aspect of what is known as '**Companion Planting**.' With this in mind I will include in this next chapter the relevant sections from my book on the subject –

Companion Planting: The Vegetable Gardeners Guide. The Role of Flowers, Herbs & Organic Thinking.

Companion Planting

Why Plants Grow Well Together

To be a little more accurate here we have to look at what we mean by 'grow well together' in other words, in what way are they beneficial to one-another's growth pattern. There are in fact three main ways that this can be so, and they are:

- Nutritional
- Protection
- Decoy

Nutrition:

In the first instance, nutrition is perhaps the first thing that springs to mind when it comes to advantageous companion planting; and indeed nutrition is of paramount importance in most cases.

Beans and peas, as in all legumes, draw in nitrogen and fix it into the soil. This in turn can provide the nutrients for corn for instance; which in turn can act as stalks for the beans. If squash is planted around the stems then this will benefit from the nitrogen, and in turn cover the ground with their broad leaves, restricting the growth of weeds and other competitors for the nutrients. This is the typical 'three sisters' approach to companion planting.

Another good example is the 'square foot' gardening approach. This is especially applicable to raised bed gardening, and is a simple rotational method of growing crops in a confined space (16 square feet), that are beneficial to each neighbour, and so produce good vegetables without the need for fertilizers.

Protection:

However there are the issues of protection against insect or herbivore predation to consider, and this goes hand in hand in many cases with the 'decoy' aspect of companion planting.

Even protection against inclement weather plays a part in companion planting. For instance some plants prefer the shade, and so can grow under the shade provided by tall plants like Tomatoes. This can also provide protection against high winds or other weather conditions, that may be detrimental to some fruit or vegetable species.

Insects:

Insects can be controlled either by using the natural insect repellent abilities of some plants to scare the insects away; or by using the natural attraction of some plants to insects like aphids for instance; in order to encourage the aphids to attack this plant rather than the one you are promoting. Marigolds for instance attract the hoverfly, who's larvae eat aphids from carrots or tomatoes.

Nasturtiums are a classic example of this, and they are widely used to draw away aphids and other destructive pests. For this reason Nasturtiums are often referred to as sacrificial or Martyr plants, as they suffer in order to protect others.

These will be cover fuller in the examples below this article, where plants that grow well together, will be listed alongside the reasons why this is the case.

It is generally accepted amongst organic growers that planting masses of the same vegetable in long rows or concentrations is a bad idea. This is because by doing so you are attracting the predators of that one species from miles around – a bit like hanging a sign up and saying 'come and get me!'

Best practice is to intersperse your crops with herbs and/or flowers that protect your crop by disguising the smells and sights that attract the insects.

Good Companions

Here is a list of plants that grow well together, with a brief explanation of just why this is the case. Although this list is not by any means an exhaustive list in itself; it only takes a little imagination to bring different species together, when you have the most basic gardening skills; and the knowledge that is contained in these notes to guide you.

Asparagus:

Best companions include: Tomato, parsley and Basil; and French marigold planted alongside will deter beetles. If on its own or just with Tomato plants, then Comfrey can be planted around as a good source of nitrogen for both plants.

Beans:

Companions include; Beetroot, cabbage, celery, carrot, cucumber, corn, squash, pea's, potatoes, radish, strawberry. Beans produce (draw from the air) nitrogen that is beneficial to the other plants
Nasturtium and rosemary can deter bean Beatles, while Marigolds can deter Mexican bean Beatles.

Cabbage Family:

Companions include; cucumber, lettuce, potato, onion, spinach, celery.
Chamomile and garlic can be grown to improve growth and flavour.

Marigolds and Nasturtium can be grown alongside to act as decoy for butterfly's and aphid pests. While mint, rosemary and sage will also deter cabbage moth and ants – as well as improve flavour.

Marigolds planted next to carrots attract hover flies, who's larvae in turn eat aphids. The smell of the marigold flowers also confuse the carrot fly

Carrots:

Good companions include beans, peas, onions, lettuce, tomato, and radish.

Including chives in the area will improve flavour and growth, while onions or leeks will distract the carrot fly by masking the scent of the carrots; as will sage or rosemary.

Celery:

Bean, tomato and cabbage family make good companions for celery.

Nasturtium, chives and garlic deters aphids and other bugs.

Corn:

Good companions are Potato, pumpkin, squash, tomato and cucumber.

French marigold deters beetles and attracts aphids from tomatoes.

Cucumber:

Good companions include, cabbage, beans, cucumber, radish, tomato.

Marigold and Nasturtium are good for attracting to themselves, aphids and beetles. Oregano is a good all round pest deterrent.

Lettuce:

Cabbage, carrot, beet, onion, and strawberry are all good companions for Lettuce.

Chives and garlic discourage aphids.

Melon:

Companions include pumpkin, radish, corn, and squash. Marigold and Nasturtium deters bugs and beetles, as does oregano.

Onions:
Good Companions include the cabbage family, beet, tomato, pepper, strawberry, peas, and chard.
Chamomile and summer savoury helps improve growth and flavour. Pigweed brings up nutrients from the subsoil, and improves conditions for the onions.

Parsley:
Good companions include asparagus, tomato and corn.

Peas:
Good companions include beans, carrot, corn and radish. Chives and onions help deter aphids, as does nasturtium. Planting mint is known to improve the health and flavour of peas.

Peppers:
Tomato, eggplant, carrot and onion are known to be good companions for peppers.

Potatoes:
Good companions include, bean, cabbage, squash and peas. Marigold makes a good general deterrent for beetles, while horseradish planted around the potato patch gives a good overall insect protection.

Pumpkin:

Melon eggplant and corn make good companions for pumpkin.
Oregano and Marigold give a good all round insect protection.

Radish:
Companions are carrot, cucumber, bean, pea, melon.
Nasturtium planted around is generally accepted to improve growth and flavour.

Squash:
Companions include melon, pumpkin, squash and tomato; while nasturtium and marigold; along with oregano, helps protect against bugs and beetles.

Strawberry:
Good companions include bean, lettuce, onion and spinach. Planting thyme around the border deters worms, while borage strengthens general resistance to disease.

Tomatoes:
Good companion plants for tomatoes include; celery, cucumber, asparagus, parsley, pepper and carrot.
Basil and dwarf marigold deter flies and aphids; mint can improve health and all round flavour.

These are some examples from popular vegetable types, and offer a guide as to what to consider for your companion garden.

The next chapter takes a brief look at what plants do not grow well together for any number of reasons.

Bad Companions

There are a few reasons why some plants should not be grown alongside others if you are considering the organic method of growing your vegetables.

I mention particularly organic, because the general idea behind companion planting is to avoid the use of chemical pesticides and fertilizers whenever possible.

Some plants should not be grown together simply because they both attract the same pests or other predators, others because they make the same demands on the soil, leading to them both producing a poor harvest. Some plants grown close together may produce a damp environment that leads to fungal or other infection.

Here are some plants to avoid planting close together if possible, when considering a companion for your veggies.

Beans:
Should not be grown in the same vicinity of garlic, shallot or onions, as they tend to stunt the growth of the beans.

Beets:
Should not be grown along with pole beans, as they stunt each other's growth.

Cabbage
Is generally thought not to do well near tomatoes, mainly because the tomato plant can shade the cabbage. Avoid planting near radishes, as they do not grow well together.

Carrots:
Avoid planting near dill as this can stunt growth. Dill and carrots both belong in the Umbelliferae family, and if allowed to flower it will cross-pollinate with the carrots. Avoid planting alongside Celery as this is from the same family.

Corn:
Where possible, avoid planting corn and tomatoes together, as they both attract the same tomato fruit-worm.

Cucumber:
Sage should be avoided near cucumber, as it generally injurious to the cucumber plant.

Peas:
Onions and garlic stunt the growth of peas.

Potatoes:
Tomatoes and potatoes should not be planted together as they attract the same blight, and use up the same nutrients from the soil.

Radish:
Avoid planting hyssop near radishes.

NOTES/MY TO-DO PAGE

Beneficial Herbs

There are many herbs that can be extremely beneficial for your companion planting. Indeed the herbs themselves can lend that extra dimension to your vegetable garden, that will complement your vegetables – and improve your cooking!

Here is a list of some popular herbs along with the benefits they may have to certain plants.

Anise:
Anise is known to benefit beans and coriander plants.

Basil:
This is known to benefit asparagus, beans, cabbage and especially tomatoes.
It can be beneficial also as a 'sacrificial' plant in that it's soft leaves tend to attract butterflies and boring insects.

Caraway:
This is an ideal herb for breaking down and conditioning poor soils. It also attracts the attention of wasps and other harmful insects, making it a good 'sacrificial' herb. Also known to benefit strawberries and peas.

Chives:
An ideal companion for carrots, as it confuses the carrot fly. Also good around peppers, potato, rhubarb, squash or tomato plants, as it deters insects – particularly aphids.

Fennel:

This makes a **poor** companion plant for just about anything – avoid planting near other plants.

Lavender:
A good companion plant for many species as it's aromatic flowers attract many beneficial, pollinating insects to the garden.
It will also deter fleas, ticks and even mice!

Mint:
This is another all-round beneficial companion for many plant species; and in particular, peas, cabbage and tomatoes.
Mint is known also to deter insects, and even mice from your plants.

Parsley:
Asparagus is known to benefit particularly well, when grown alongside parsley; but carrots, cor, sweet peppers are also good companions.
Avoid planting near mint or lettuce.

Peppermint:
A good companion as it attracts beneficial insects and repels ants, aphids and cabbage fly.

Rosemary:
Beans, broccoli, cabbage, and hot peppers all benefit from being planted alongside rosemary.
Planting carrots and pumpkins nearby is not advised as rosemary makes a poor companion for them.

Thyme:

Many plants such as cabbage, eggplant, potatoes and strawberries will benefit from planting thyme nearby; as it attracts many beneficial insects to the garden including honey bees.

It is also accredited with chasing off tomato hornworm, cabbage worms and flea beetles.

Typical Configuration of SFG with Herbs & Veg

South Facing

BASIL (4)	BEET (9)	BEET (9)	LAVENDER (1)
RADISH (16)	ONIONS (4)	ONIONS (4)	RADISH (16)
CHIVES (16)	CARROTS (16)	CARROTS (16)	CHIVES (16)
BEANS (8)	BEANS (8)	PEAS (8)	PEAS (8)

Organic Pest Control

Controlling garden pests using organic methods does require a bit of 'thinking outside the box' and forward planning. It has as much to do with prevention or distraction, as with anything else. Again there are organic pest control sprays that you can purchase if necessary, however a good recipe for your own spray is simply to get some insecticidal soap and add about a half cup to one bucket of water. Mix thoroughly and add to your hand sprayer to apply to your plants. This is very effective against aphids, greenfly, blackfly leafhoppers and others. If you cannot get your hands on insecticidal soap, then try good old liquid washing up liquid in an emergency.

Another way of controlling pests, is to use the rotational crop growing method described in the previous chapter. This works by simply not allowing the pests and diseases that would build up in the soil, if you grow the same crops every year in the same place. By changing the growing pattern you also stop the chance of infestation from the same sources.

Deterring slugs:

Slugs can be deterred from getting near your vegetables, by the use of copper tape or even paint. They cannot cross copper as it reacts with their slime, so stopping them in their tracts. Scattering salt around your pots or raised bed can also be a great deterrent, as this acts like acid to slugs – unpleasant but effective. Do not let the salt get near your plants though! Slugs can also be collected by sinking a jam-jar into the ground and half filling with beer. This is called a beer trap, and is something that has been used quite effectively for centuries. Slugs love beer and will head for the jar, drowning in the beer. Traps have to be cleaned out regularly though – which is not the most pleasant of jobs admittedly!

Carrot fly:

Carrot fly can be deterred by a mixture of companion planting and creating barriers. By planting garlic or onions around your carrots, you are effectively masking the scent of the carrot from the dreaded carrot fly, which is attracted by the smell from the foliage. Covering the carrots with a fine insect mesh or gardeners fleece can prevent them from gaining entry to the plants.

Finally, as the carrot fly is known to be a low flyer then it is possible to keep it away by simply growing your carrots in a raised situation such as a raised bed. Either that or surround your carrots with a two foot high plywood fence to stop the fly.

Aphid control:

As mentioned in the earlier paragraph, aphids can be sprayed with your insecticidal mix or they can be controlled by the introduction of ladybugs if your vegetables are growing in an enclosed situation such as a greenhouse. Ladybugs love to snack on aphids and so are ideal for the purpose of organic pest control.

There is however a downside – if they eat all the aphids, then they will go hungry, and so you cannot effectively get rid of all the aphids as you would hope to do with spraying.

Companion planting with marigolds around your tomato plants for instance is known to be quite effective against green and blackfly, as they hate the strong smell of them apparently.

Cabbage looper:

Again the cabbage looper caterpillar can be treated by spraying with you insecticidal soap mixture. However it is probably easier to cover all your cabbage plants with gardeners fleece. This still lets through the water and about 85% of the sun's rays, and so is very effective against any flying moths, butterflies etc.

Top Tips:

- Save growing space in your SFG by growing Companion plants for insect control such as Marigolds or Nasturtiums in containers placed around your SFG instead of within the growing area itself.
- A small 'fence' two feet high and covered with gardeners fleece will protect your carrots from the dreaded carrot fly.
- Plan out your herbs to compliment the vegetables in the squares, Chives for instance keep the fly off your carrots and Basil loves beans, carrots and tomatoes.
- Keep a plan of your SFG planting to be sure you do not repeat yourself the next season. Excel is excellent for this purpose if you can use it.
- Get the kids involved! This is a great way to introduce children to gardening as the size of the area does not overwhelm them, and things like pulling weeds is easy for them in the loose soil.
- Cover seedlings with gardeners fleece for the first few days to harden them off when transplanting outside.

Crop Rotation:

As mentioned earlier, proper rotation of the vegetables you plan to grow plays an important role in the successful SFG. As each crop or vegetable plants reaches the end of its life, then be sure that you consider a different plant to grow in its place.

This process of crop rotation ensures that nutrient depletion from growing the same crops over and over again on the same piece of land does not occur, but instead the land is continually refreshed and kept nutrient rich by careful management and effective crop rotation.

Rotating the crops in this way also plays a part in organic pest control as any soil-borne disease or pest infestation that may be present in the ground after the harvest of a particular plant, will hopefully not be a threat to the new vegetables you are about to plant in the space previously occupied.

To further understand this, there are certain rules regarding the management of your vegetables which is based around the principles below.

Vegetables are ranked into 4 main categories, and they are..

1. **Legumes**: french beans, peas, runner beans, broad beans
2. **Root vegetables**: radish, carrot, potato, onion, garlic, beetroot, swede, sweet potato, shallots, leeks
3. **Leafy greens**: spinach, cabbage, cauliflower, broccoli, lettuce, spinach

4. **Fruit-bearing**: tomato, sweetcorn, cucumber, squash, pumpkin, courgette, strawberry, pepper, aubergine, water melon

You must also bear in mind that plants also belong to 'families.' For instance it is not clear from this list, but tomato and potato are in fact in the same family and so will attract the same pests and use up the same soil nutrients. This of course means that they should be planted separately wherever possible.

As the goal of proper crop management means that you do not wish to deplete the soil nutrients by planting vegetables with the same requirements either together or following one after the other, it is important also to know the families to which they belong.

Brassicas (Cabbage Family):
Brussels sprout, broccoli, all varieties of cabbage, kohl rabi, cauliflower, kale, pak choi, radish, rocket, swede, turnip.

Legumes (Bean & Pea Family):
Mange tout, pea, borlotti, runner, French and broad beans.

Solanaceae (Potato & Tomato Family):
Aubergine, potato, peppers, tomato.

Umbelliferae (carrot & Root Family):
Celery, celeriac, fennel, carrot, coriander, parsnip, parsley, dill.

Alliums (Onion Family):
Garlic, shallot, chive, leek and all varieties of onion.

Cucurbits (Squash & Marrow Family):
Cucumber, courgette, marrow, melon, pumpkin, squash.

Chenopodiaceae (Beetroot Family):
Beetroot, perpetual spinach, Swiss chard, spinach,

Miscellaneous Plants:
All fruit, mint, oregano, rosemary, sage, basil, lettuce, cress, Jerusalem artichoke, sweetcorn, asparagus, okra, salsify, corn salad, chicory

General Guidelines/summary :
Brassicas follow Legumes:
The general rule in crop rotation is that Brassicas follow Legumes. This means that you would sow crops such as cauliflower, cabbage and kale on soil previously occupied with peas and beans. This means that the Brassicas will benefit from the nitrogen rich soil that the Legumes have left behind.

Roots don't like rich soil:
Root vegetables should not be planted in very rich or over fertilized soil, as the leafy part of the veg will bloom at the expense of the edible root itself. Whenever possible, plant parsnips for instance the season after more demanding crops such as brassicas have broken down the rich soil.

NOTES/MY TO-DO PAGE

Planting & Growing

Plant Support:

There are many plants that require support of some kind, especially when the fruits begin to grow and gain weight thereby adding strain to the plant stem.

There are also many ways to achieve this – although they mainly focus around canes, cages or garden twine. The basic principle is the same, and it's not complicated!

Check out the diagrams & pictures below to get an idea of what would suit your need best.

The picture above is a typical cane and string trellis work that will support many climbing plants such as beans, peas and tomato plants.

For plants that bear heavier fruits such as marrow, zucchini cucumber etc; then you have to increase the load-bearing capacity – which basically just means using heavier string and supports.

Another option is to use heavy farmers 4 inch mesh or other wire fencing products, to form a cage that will support many different plants. This wire is simply turned into shape and tied with thinner wire to prevent springing. Cut in such a way as to leave protruding wire at the end so that you can easily secure the cage into the soil.

These cages in turn are usually self-supporting but can be easily held in place by 1 or 2 canes. In this example above you will also see an example of an irrigation system simply formed using plumber's pipe and drip feeders. There are many irrigation systems available commercially to choose from.

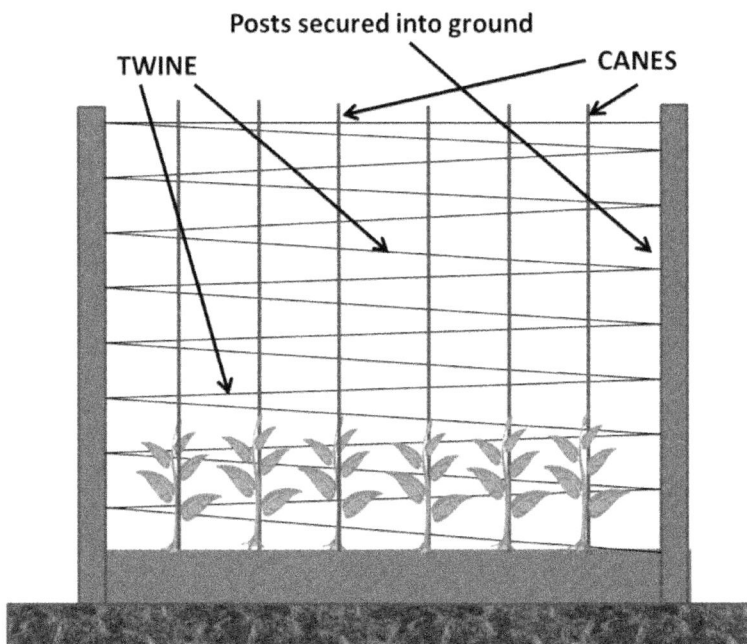

The diagram above represents a typical trellis support that can be used for many types of climbing plants. Canes take most of the weight, whilst garden twine is tied into eye-fixings on the posts to help spread and support the plants.

This type can be placed at the back of the SFG or depending on your requirements you may choose to try the same trellis but in the 'wigwam' style. Below you can see an end view of what that would look like.

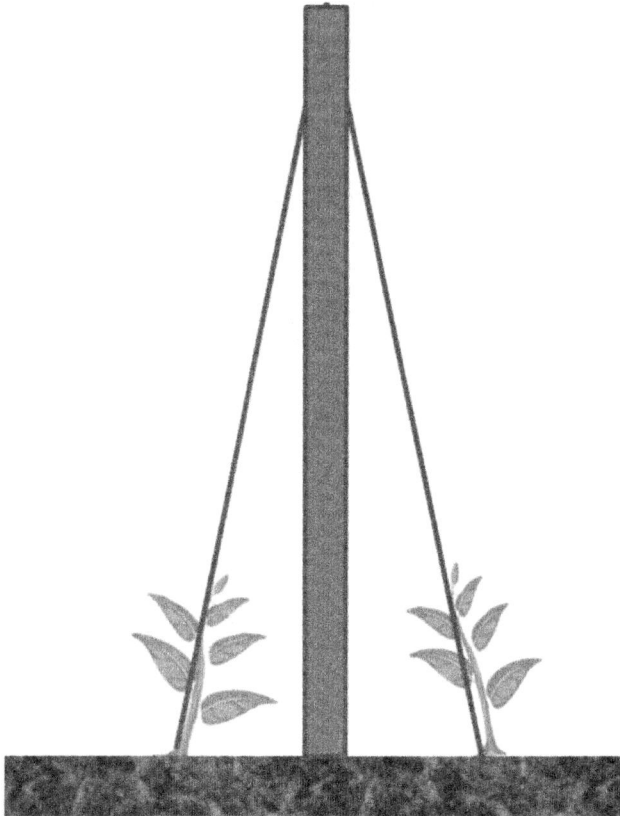

About Planting Zones:

When it comes down to timing the planting of your seeds or seedlings, this very much depends on where you live as times and seasons of course vary widely even within the United States itself.

For this reason it is impossible to give exact months for planting in the following list of plants, so instead I have erred on the side of vagueness, and trust in your own local knowledge as to the correct planting time according to which zone you reside in.

With that in mind I have included two Plant Hardiness zone maps – one for the US and one for the UK – that may help you decide which plants may thrive and which will not. The fact is though that there is no substitute for local knowledge, and I would encourage you to seek out information from your local sources such as garden centres, keen gardeners or the internet, as to which vegetables will thrive where you live.

I will point out however that these zone maps do not take into consideration the extremes of summer weather, humidity, days of frost or length of days – each of which may have a profound bearing on the vegetables you are seeking to grow.

With that said; the map below is distributed by the United States Department of Agriculture. By checking out your zone you can at least be a little more informed as to what you can successfully grow in your region.

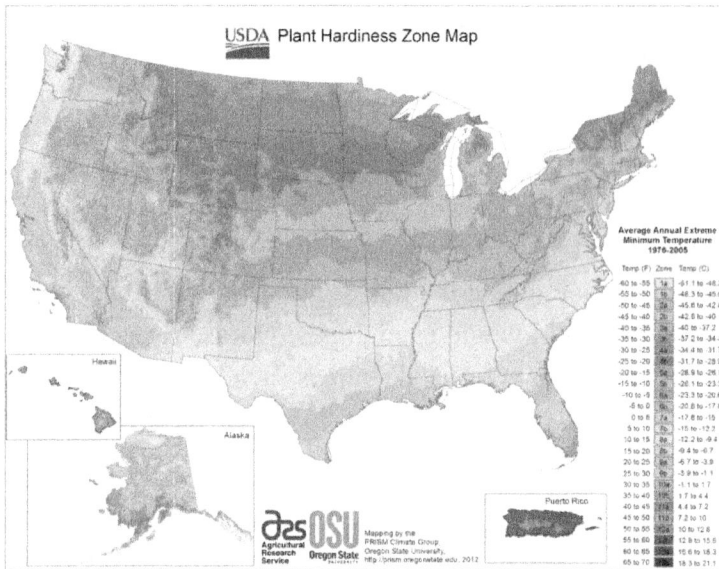

An enlarged map of the temperatures

Average Annual Extreme Minimum Temperature 1976-2005

Temp (F)	Zone	Temp (C)
-60 to -55	1a	-51.1 to -48.3
-55 to -50	1b	-48.3 to -45.6
-50 to -45	2a	-45.6 to -42.8
-45 to -40	2b	-42.8 to -40
-40 to -35	3a	-40 to -37.2
-35 to -30	3b	-37.2 to -34.4
-30 to -25	4a	-34.4 to -31.7
-25 to -20	4b	-31.7 to -28.9
-20 to -15	5a	-28.9 to -26.1
-15 to -10	5b	-26.1 to -23.3
-10 to -5	6a	-23.3 to -20.6
-5 to 0	6b	-20.6 to -17.8
0 to 5	7a	-17.8 to -15
5 to 10	7b	-15 to -12.2
10 to 15	8a	-12.2 to -9.4
15 to 20	8b	-9.4 to -6.7
20 to 25	9a	-6.7 to -3.9
25 to 30	9b	-3.9 to -1.1
30 to 35	10a	-1.1 to 1.7
35 to 40	10b	1.7 to 4.4
40 to 45	11a	4.4 to 7.2
45 to 50	11b	7.2 to 10
50 to 55	12a	10 to 12.8
55 to 60	12b	12.8 to 15.6
60 to 65	13a	15.6 to 18.3
65 to 70	13b	18.3 to 21.1

More detailed information on these planting zones can be found on their website at http://planthardiness.ars.usda.gov/PHZMWeb/Default.aspx For my readers in the United Kingdom the following Planting Zone map will apply.

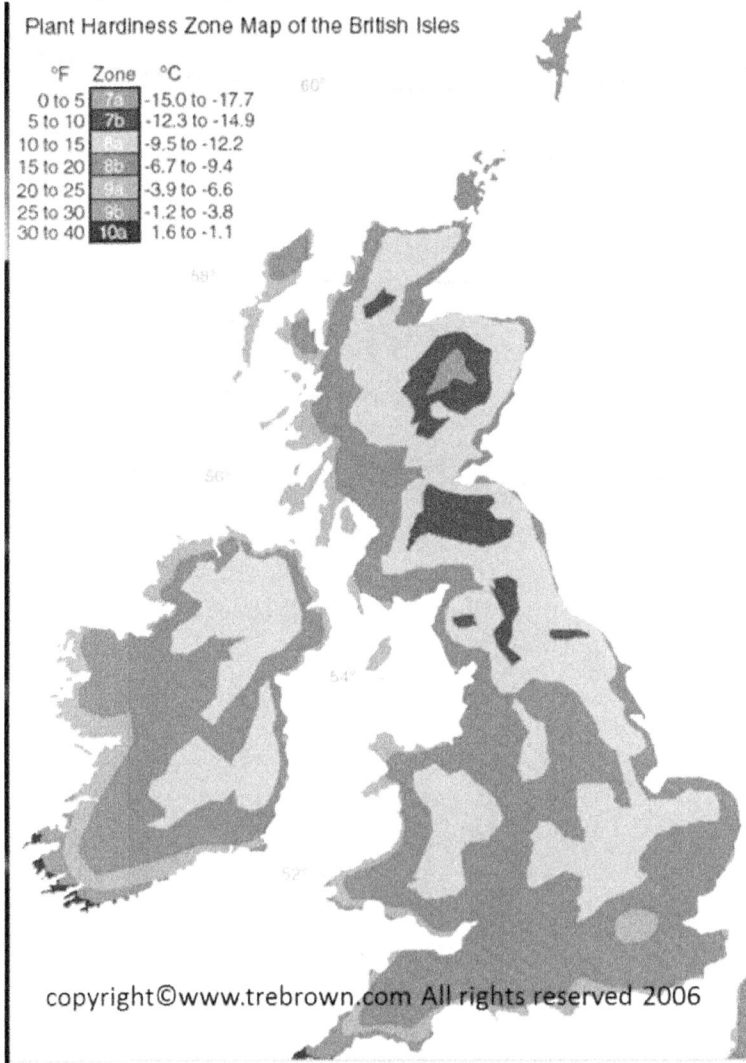

Plant Hardiness Zone Map of the British Isles

°F	Zone	°C
0 to 5	7a	-15.0 to -17.7
5 to 10	7b	-12.3 to -14.9
10 to 15	8a	-9.5 to -12.2
15 to 20	8b	-6.7 to -9.4
20 to 25	9a	-3.9 to -6.6
25 to 30	9b	-1.2 to -3.8
30 to 40	10a	1.6 to -1.1

Map courtesy of www.trebrown.com

As the United Kingdom climate is greatly changed by the activity of the Gulf Stream (North Atlantic Stream), it is able to grow vegetables that would otherwise be difficult considering its Northern latitude.

Popular Vegetables For Your SFG

This list of vegetables and their growing conditions takes into account the superior make-up of the soil already discussed for your SFG – conditions that will provide most (if not all) of the nutrients required for the individual plants.

Liquid Organic Fertilizer as discussed earlier, as well as a compost top-up can be applied as the individual plants mature and produce their fruits.

Insect Control: Refer to the section on companion planting and pest control, for effective Organic insect and disease control methods.

Watering & Irrigation:
It is taken as wrote that all plants, both seedlings and adults need water to grow! For that reason I have not laboured the point in this following section. All seeds must be sufficiently watered upon planting. Where extra care must be taken in this area however I have added a small note in the Plant Care sections.

***

Asparagus:

Asparagus is a vegetable that requires more than the usual patience to grow, as it will not start producing for 2-3 years after planting. Thereafter however you can have Asparagus shoots for up to 20 years or more – so it is worth the wait in the long term!

It thrives best in areas that have long cold winters as it is a cool-season early crop.

Planting:

Asparagus is grown from 'crowns' that are planted in the early spring. These are 1 year old plants that can be purchased from your local garden centre or other commercial supplier.

Asparagus requires good nutrition and drainage to prosper well which makes any king of SFG or Raised Bed ideal for them.

To plant your Asparagus first dig a round hole in your soil about 6 inches deep and the area of your square – 1 plant per square. Spread out the roots of your young plant and lay into the hole, covering to the top of the plant with the soil; water thoroughly.

As the plant begins to grow then slowly form a mound around the stem leaving it protruding a couple of inches above the soil.

Plant Care:

Do not harvest in the first year but instead at the end of the season cut away the dead foliage and re-cover with fresh mulch.

The second year keep the bed thickly mulched and prevent weeds from running amok!

By the third year you may start to harvest your crop.

Harvesting:

The season for harvesting Asparagus is very short – only about 3 weeks – so you must stay alert. Cut the stems that are about 6 inches in length and the thickness of a pencil. When the harvesting is over then allow the ferns to grow and die on the heap to replenish your crop for next season. Surplus asparagus can be frozen and used throughout the rest of the summer.

Beets:

Beets are a good choice for gardeners in the Northern climate as they grow well in the cooler conditions. An excellent long-season crop as they are even able to survive frosty temperatures. Will prosper well in high phosphorous levels, but high nitrogen may result in excessive leafiness and small bulbs.

Planting:

Seeds can be planted 1-2 inches apart and ½ inch deep, but wait until soil reaches 50 degrees before sowing.

If temperature allows, planting can begin late March/April and continue until late in the season. Plantings can be spaced around 20 days apart to allow for Beets throughout the season.

A good crop for late – even winter crops in zone 9 or above.

Plant Care:

Thin out the plants when they reach about 2 inches high by pinching them off at the base, or snip with shears so not to disturb the ground. Leave a gap of around 3-4 inches between plants.

Harvesting:

Beets are usually ready for harvesting in 50-70 days, though they can be harvested any time after the bulb appears. They can be left longer but will become tougher as they grow, and slightly woody.

The leaves are also delicious and make a good addition to salad dishes.

Apart from storing in a cool dry place; Beets can be pickled, frozen or canned to preserve them.

Broccoli:

This is a cool-season crop which can germinate in temperatures as low as 40 degrees F, making it an ideal early starter for your veggie plot.

Planting:
For early spring planning, plant seeds or seedlings 2-3 weeks before the last frosts of spring. For Autumn plants then plant about 80-100 days before the first winter frosts. In your SFG plant 3 seeds ½ inch deep, close together in the centre of the square then choose the stronger of the bunch when they are about 3-4 inches high, and remove the other two.

Plant Care:
Although this is a moisture-loving plant, be careful not to get the heads wet when watering.
This is a shallow rooted plant so care must be taken when weeding around the stem that you do not disturb the roots.

Harvesting:
Broccoli should be cut about 6 inches from the head of the plant at the stem when the heads are still tight and firm.
More will grow from the side-shoots of the plant, meaning that one plant will usually produce several heads of Broccoli over the growing season.
Can be stored in a refrigerator for several days, and can be kept for up to one year if blanched and frozen.

Green Beans:

Bush beans and Pole beans (usually referred to as **green beans**) are a great addition to any kitchen table, and if picked while still young can be a tasty snack straight from the plant.

Planting:

Not a good plant to transplant as a seedling; green beans are best sown directly into the soil soon after the last frost of spring when soil temperature is around 50 degrees F. Plant seeds 1 inch deep and 3 inches apart. Make sure that you have a trellis or canes in place to support your plants as they grow -

4 – 8 plants per square can be grown in your SFG. Plant 2-3 weeks apart if you want a regular crop over the season.

Plant Care:

Beans are a great starter crop as they are fairly easy to care for. The usual ground care with regard to weeding etc (not a big problem with a SFG) is required, and watering should be done on a sunny day if possible to prevent over-soaking of the foliage.

Harvesting:

Carefully snap or cut off the beans from the stem before they are fully developed, this will assure best flavour and beans that are not to tough.

Store in the refrigerator in an air-tight container for best results. For longer storage blanch and freeze; they can also be pickled or canned.

Brussels Sprouts:

This is the kind of vegetable that you either love or hate! Some folks find them quite sweet, while others (like myself) find them as bitter as heck! All down to an enzyme in the taste buds apparently. They also are believed to possess potent anti-cancer properties – for which reason alone I would recommend including them in your growing plans.

Planting:
Plant seeds indoors about ½ inch deep and 2-3 inches apart, about 6 weeks before the last frost of spring. Thin out the weakest and transplant into your SFG, 1 plant per square.

Plant Care:
This vegetable is very undemanding regarding on-going care, and as long as it has sufficient nutrients and water, there is little else to do except wait for the harvest!

Harvesting:
Sprouts are ready to harvest from the stalk when they reach 1 inch in diameter. Store in the fridge or a cool place for a few days before use, and do not wash until ready for consumption.
Sprouts can last around 3-5 weeks if kept just above freezing temperature.

Cabbage:

Cabbage is a popular vegetable with many varieties offering opportunities for many different growing conditions and taste preferences. Rich in iron, it likes cool temperatures and so is best planted early spring and fall.

Planting:

Planting pattern is similar to that for the Brussels Sprouts, by planting seeds indoors about 8 weeks before the last spring frost. Transplant 1 plant into each square of your SFG about two weeks before the last frost.

Plant Care:

Keep soil moist and watch out for the cabbage butterfly! Cabbage seems particularly prone to caterpillars so check out the companion planting section for pest control methods.

Harvesting:

When the cabbage has formed a suitably firm head then it is ready for harvesting – usually in about 65 days or so. Remove by cutting at the base of the head, but leave the stem planted along with the outer leaves. The plant will then send up fresh shoots to form new heads.

Leave just 3 or 4 of these heads to develop and they will form miniature cabbages.

Make sure your cabbage is not wet, before wrapping in cling-film and storing in a cool place for no more than two weeks.

Carrots:

One of the most popular of vegetables, carrots prefer a light sandy soil, and although resistant to most diseases, they will suffer badly if the dreaded carrot fly is around.

Protect by planting them surrounded by chives or onions to disguise the carrot smell from the fly.

Planting:
Make sure that the soil is free of stones or obstructions as this will cause the carrot to 'fork' or split out. Plant seeds ½ inch or so deep a few weeks before the last spring frost. Thin out by snipping the plants with scissors rather than pulling, when the carrot foliage is about two inches high. Create a space 2-3 inches apart.

Plant Care:
Keep free of weeds but be careful not to disturb the soil around the carrot, and make things easy for the dreaded carrot fly!
Flavour is enhanced after the first frost, so better leave harvesting them until after that. Cover with mulch and leave in the soil if you plan harvesting them later.

Harvesting:
After around 10 weeks carrots are ready for consumption. They can be left in the ground if protected from frost, or

they can be lifted, the tops twisted off and the tuber cleaned. Thereafter the carrots can be kept in a sealed plastic bag and stored in the fridge; or they can be buried in some moist sand until ready for use.

Cauliflower:

This is one of the more difficult crops to grow, especially if you live in a warm climate as Cauliflower prefers constant temperatures in the 60's.

This makes it a more specialized crop, usually grown commercially in climates that suit it well.

Planting:

Cauliflowers should be planted where they can get at least 6 hours full sun per day. Seeds can be planted under cover about 6 weeks before the last frost – about the same time as cabbage. Plant seeds ½ inch into the soil and transplant when they are about 4 inches high.

Alternatively plant your young plants about 2-3 weeks before the frost is finished.

One cauliflower per square is all you need for your SFG.

Plant Care:

Cauliflower needs to be watered regularly in order to grow well – not overwatered! Just keep the soil around the bas moist. As the white head begins to grow to 3-4 inches, take the outer leaves and tie them over the head to protect from the elements – a light rubber band will do nicely – this is known as 'Blanching' and it will keep the head a nice white colour.

Harvesting:

Plants are usually ready to harvest 7-15 days after blanching, usually at about 6 inches in diameter.

Cut the head from the stem with a sharp knife, retaining some of the leaves to protect it. Can be stored in a cool place for around a week; to keep for longer blanch before freezing or pickle the heads.

Corn:

Sweet corn is a delicious crop well loved by many. Roasted over hot coals or boiled in water, it is traditionally served piping hot covered with melted butter.. mmmm.

It is a warm-weather vegetable and as such requires a long frost-free growing season to reach its full potential.

Planting:
This is a crop best planted from seed directly into your SFG. Plant 3 seeds per square about 1 inch deep and 2-3 weeks after the last frost when the soil temperature is 60 degrees or over to be sure of germination. Cover with gardeners fleece to protect from cold if any late cold-snap should arise.

As Corn is wind-pollinated, planting in clumps of 3 plants at a time helps in this respect.

Plant Care:
Corn has very shallow roots so be sure to keep well watered especially as they start to grow the corn heads. Well drained yet moisture retentive soil (as you should already have in your SFG) make ideal conditions for growing Sweetcorn.

Care must be taken not to damage the shallow roots when weeding around your Corn plants.

Harvesting:

Corn is ready to harvest when the tassels turn brown and the cob is full. Remove by simply pulling the cob down and twisting from the plant.

Sweetcorn will lose its flavour quickly after picking and so is best consumed immediately, or frozen for later.

Cucumber:

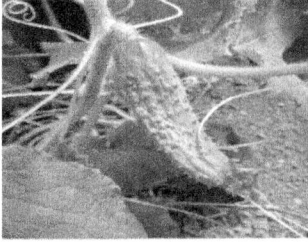

A popular salad vegetable, the cucumber is a fast growing climbing plant that definitely prefers the heat. Each plant will provide a number of fresh cucumbers throughout the growing season.

Planting:

Make sure that the plant is exposed to full sun, and decide before hand if you would like to allow the plant to climb up a trellis or grow on the ground. This is especially important in your SFG layout, as a trellis grown plant would be best placed at the back of the SFG so that it does not 'shade-out' the other crops.

Plant 1 or 2 seeds or seedlings to the square.

If planting from seed then grow inside in a warm place (65 degrees is needed for germination) and do not plant outside until at least two weeks after the last frost.

Cucumber is very susceptible to the frost so I would keep a fleece covering at hand to cover for the first week or so after planting.

Plant Care:

If your cucumbers are going to be lying on the ground, then lay them on a covering or straw to protect from the wet soil. Hanging Cucumbers may have to be supported on the vine.

Cucumbers need constant watering as inconsistent watering can result in a small, bitter plant. To avoid over watering, a quick tip is to stick your finger into the soil and if it is dry beyond the first joint then water is needed.

Harvesting:

Harvest your cucumbers regularly to maintain a healthy crop when they reach 6 inches and over; or if pickling them around 2 inches.

Keep picking them as they grow on the vine as the vine will stop producing if they are not picked, and those that remain will become tough and slightly bitter.

As they are 90% water, cucumbers are better stored wrapped tightly in plastic film. They will last at least 7-10 days in this condition if stored in a cool place.

Leeks:

This is a most popular vegetable, ideal for stews and casseroles. The leek is a member of the onion family, but without the bulb and has a gentler, sweeter taste.

Planting:

Nutritional demands are the same as for onions. Seeds should be planted in a shallow trench indoors, a full 12 weeks before the last frost, and the seedlings thinned out and planted 9 to the square in your SFG.

Plant by making a hole in your soil about 2-3 inches deep and place your seedling down into the hole. Fill and press the soil lightly around it. As it grows earth-up the soil as this will produce a longer white stem for consumption. Alternatively allow the leek to grow up through a cardboard tube 4 inches tall specially placed over it for the occasion – this will have the same effect as earthing-up the soil.

Plant Care:

Leeks are a very hardy crop not so prone to insect or disease attack and take little care once planted. Apart from gentle weeding and keeping sufficiently watered, there is little to be done but watch them grow!

Harvesting:

Once mature after about 100 days or so, the leeks can be lifted for consumption or left in the ground for later, as long as they are protected from severe frost by covering with fleece.

Leeks soon dry out and so are best consumed a few days after lifting, otherwise leave them in the ground or blanch them prior to freezing.

Onions:

Onions the delight of every chef, in fact I wonder how we could survive without them! A cold-season crop, the onion is a hardy vegetable that is relatively easy to grow and undemanding regarding care and protection from disease or insects.

Planting:

Onions require nitrogen rich, loose soil in which to prosper – conditions that suit SF gardeners just fine!

The recommended way to plant onions is to buy onion sets rather than seeds, but if seeds are preferred then start indoors about 4-5 weeks before transplanting.

Young plants or sets should be planted 4 to a square, making sure that they are not under the shade of larger plants.

Sink 1/3rd of the bulb into the soil, then press lightly to firm them in.

Plant Care:

Onions need little care, however as they grow you may find that they will rise out of the soil and so occasionally need to be lightly pressed down again until the root system gets fully established.

Watch out also for blackbirds and crows that will occasionally pull the unestablished plants out of the ground, leaving them on the surface to wither and die.

If the onion sends up flower stalks then this means that it has 'bolted' and is no use. Remove from the bed and discard.

Harvesting:

Onions are ready to harvest when the tops start to become yellow and brown. At this stage you can encourage the process by folding over the stems. After a few days carefully lift the onions and lay on the surface of the ground to dry out. Do this before the really cool weather arrives as the mature onion may spoil in bad weather.

Allow to dry for 2-3 weeks before considering storing them. This can be done by leaving them on the dry ground, or in bad weather lay them out on a table-top indoors. When the plants stems have dried out they are best braided together and hung up in a cool dry place, for use throughout the winter months.

Peas:

Two of the most popular peas for growing are the Snow Peas and the Snap peas. Both have edible pods as well as peas, and when harvested promptly are sweet and delicious either cooked or straight from the vine.

This is a great vegetable to start the kids on as it is easy to grow and fast growing – a great boon to impatient children!

Planting:

Peas are easily grown from seeds planted outdoors about 4 weeks before the last spring frost. Seeds will germinate at 45 degrees F. Plant up to 8 seeds 1 inch deep, into a square that has been prepared with canes, trellis, cage or other support for the peas to climb up.

Naturally these are best planted to the back of the SFG to allow the sunlight to get to your other, shorter plants.

Plant Care:

Care is fairly straight-forward with peas; simply water and remove any weeds, check for insect predations (Aphids and Bean Beatles tend to like peas). Harvesting itself is part of the plant care for this vegetable as it will produce more pods when harvested regularly.

Harvesting:

Pluck the vine regularly using both hands to prevent damaging the stem. This is best done early morning after the dew had dried off as this is when they are most crisp and flavoursome.

Peas are best kept wrapped in a paper bag before placing in the fridge or another cool place. They will remain 'fresh' for up to 7 days like this.

Peas freeze well and can be dried by removing peas from the pods and drying out for winter soups and stews.

Sweet Bell Peppers:

Peppers come in many shapes, colours and sizes, hot or sweet – and modern-day chefs would be lost without them! A simple plant to grow if you have warm enough conditions (average 70 degrees F.) Bell Peppers are a great addition to your vegetable garden.

Planting:

Peppers will not survive in ground temperatures below 65 degrees F. So if you want to grow them outdoors this is the minimum requirement; in cooler climates it is best to grow in a greenhouse environment,

Plant 1 or 2 plants close together per square in your SFG, along with sufficient support in the form of wire cage or canes; as the plants will tend to droop with the weight of the peppers as they grow.

Seeds should be grown about 3-4 to a pot and the weakest discarded, before transplanting the healthy plants to your SFG after the spring frosts are well clear.

Plant Care:

This is a thirsty plant so be sure to water regularly especially if you live an exceptional hot dry climate.

Make sure the fruits are properly supported and that the plant is not struggling under the weight.

Be careful when weeding around the base of the plants as this can damage the shallow roots.

Watch out for Aphids and Flea beetles and blossom-end rot - which occurs when calcium is low – usually because of irregular insufficient watering practices.

Harvesting:
Peppers grow in sweetness and flavour the longer you leave them on the plant, and increase in their vitamin C content. To remove peppers, snip the stems with a pair of scissors to avoid tearing the plant stem.
Peppers will store in a fridge for 7-10 days in a plastic bag.

Potatoes:

This is the staple vegetable for millions worldwide and comes in many different varieties. A vegetable for the cooler climate, potatoes come as early, mid or late planting varieties and is the World's 4th largest food crop.

Home-grown potatoes are renowned for being much tastier than store-bought, and picked fresh from the ground they cannot be beaten!

Planting:

Potatoes are planted from seed potatoes that are specially grown to be disease-free and to provide consistent healthy plants.

Although you can easily grow potatoes from potato peelings that have at least 1 eye on them, it is best to plant the whole seed tuber as peelings are likely to rot before they start to germinate.

After choosing the variety that best suits your region or culinary tastes, place your potatoes in a cool dark place until the first shoots start to appear (4-6 weeks).

After the last frost has left, place one potato per square into your SFG, into a hole 6 inches deep, being careful not to break off the early shoots, then cover with the soil. As the potato grows and breaks the surface, pile compost around the shoot to encourage further upward growth. If a late frost is forecast be ready to cover the young plant with gardeners fleece or other protection.

Potatoes will grow from the stem so it is good practice to encourage this upward growth. This is the reason that growing potatoes in a wire cage, bin or other receptacle can yield great results!

Plant Care:

As the plant reaches the flowering stage and the young tubers are growing, it is important to begin 'hilling' your spuds. This is a process where you pile up extra compost or humus around the base of your plant, and make sure that none of the tubers are exposed to the daylight – this will cause them to go green and inedible.

You will need to repeat this process regularly during the growing season.

Harvesting:

Although they can be dug up earlier if you desire small tender spuds; harvesting begins when the leaves have turned yellow and begin to die. Choose a fine dry day and carefully dig up your harvest, being careful not to damage the tubers.

Potatoes should be stored in a cool dark place, away from apples which will cause them to rot owing to the ethylene gas apples produce.

Do not wash the potatoes prior to storing as this reduces their storage life, just clean away any remaining dirt and store together in wooden boxes when the potatoes are dry –

do not store if the surface of the tubers are wet otherwise they are liable to rot.

Watch out for signs of early or late blight, usually brought on by a bout of hot humid weather. This causes dark brown/yellow spots to appear, well before flowering has finished, quickly resulting in the destruction of the stems and introducing rot into the tubers. If caught in time then the crop should be harvested, tubers checked and the foliage taken away and preferably burned to prevent further infection – do not use in the compost bin!

If the tubers themselves are infected you will see a dark brown stain running through them when cut in half with a knife. Check a few of the spuds and if the potato flesh is clear then you may at least have salvaged some of the harvest.

Tomatoes:

Although botanically a fruit, the tomato is widely known as a vegetable by cooks and as such is probably the most loved *vegetable* in the garden, and varieties are numerous to say the least – over 7,500!

Tomatoes are a warm-weather plant that need at least 6-8 hours sunshine per day at temperatures between 70-85 degrees F.

Planting:
Once you have chosen your variety, whether an Heirloom vine tomato or Hybrid bush tomato it is time to get planting. Tomatoes are usually transplanted from seedlings bought at the garden center, but can be grown from seed planted indoors at least 6 weeks before the last frosts. When transplanting into your SFG; harden off the young plants first by covering with fleece to protect from late chill, and transplant only when soil has begun to warm in the spring sunshine.
Plant just one tomato plant into a square with a support cane or cage to support your plant, and water well.

Plant Care:
As the plant grows, nip off the side shoots that appear and tie your plant to the support. When the first fruit start to appear after the blooms have gone, feed one ladle of

organic tea every second day and increase to once daily as more fruits appear.

Water well especially as more fruit starts to grow, but do not over-water as this can rot the base of the stems.

Heritage vine plants can grow to around 6 feet or more, and produce an abundance of nutrient-sucking leaves; I tend to snip away the leaves on the bottom 3 feet of the plant and leave only the upper half of the plant with foliage other than the fruit bunches. This increases the nutrients that are used to produce fruit instead of leaves.

Tomatoes are prone to attack from both insect and fungus so it is wise to include companion planting practices to help reduce the risk of either.

Aphids, white-fly and Tomato Hornworm can be a particular threat.

Over humidity or soaking the leaves of the plant in particular can lead to fungal disease and tomato blight.

Harvesting:
Tomatoes are best eaten within days of plucking in order to get the best flavour possible; however if storing simply place in a paper bag and keep stem-up in a cool dark place. Contrary to popular belief green tomatoes do not ripen well on a window sill – they are more prone to rotting.

Best time to pick is when the tomato is firm and bright red (or yellow?) in color – depending on the variety of course.

They can be kept in the fridge for a few days, but in doing so you will lose much of the natural tomato flavour.

Zucchini (Courgette)

Also known as the Summer Squash, the Zucchini is a most versatile vegetable, ideal for stews or casseroles as it absorbs flavours fantastically. Just to confuse the issue it is also referred to as a Courgette in some areas.

A warm weather vegetable it is prone to excesses of heat or frost, but if properly cared for will produce an abundant crop of delicious fruits.

Planting:
Seeds should be planted indoors 2-3 weeks before the last of the spring frosts, and should not be transplanted outdoors until the frosts have gone – protect young plants with garden fleece for the first 2 weeks or so.
Soil temperature must be 60 degrees F for the Zucchini to grow, so be sure to plant in full sunshine.

Plant Care:
As the fruits start to grow, water well and any fruit laying on the surface protect with a layer of straw or dry mulch to prevent rotting.
Apply some organic tea as the first fruits begin to swell.
Be sure that the flowers are pollinated properly either by bees or manually using a fine brush or Q-tip. Lack of fruit when the plant has produced flowers is a sure sign of bad pollination.

Watch out for pests such as Aphids, Cucumber Beetle and Squash Bugs.

Harvesting:

Although it may be tempting to grow huge zucchini, especially as they do grow quickly, it is best to harvest them when they get to about 6 inches or so if you want to get the best flavour and tender fruits from them. Zucchini can be frozen if blanched in boiling water for about 3 minutes. Alternatively they can be stored for around ten days in the refrigerator.

***

From The Author

The ability to grow your own vegetables no matter how limited the space you have at your disposal (within reason), has led to a huge interest in 'no-dig' gardening techniques.

That and the fact that the crop yield can be significantly increased owing to the intensive methods employed with these methods, will no doubt ensure that this interest continues apace!

Square Foot Gardening, Raised Bed Gardening, Container Gardening and even growing vegetables in Straw Bales, means that all the family can get involved in this gardening 'revolution.'

We sincerely hope that you have enjoyed reading the information contained within this book, and if you have not already done so – put the ideas into practice!

If you would like to leave a comment or review on Amazon We would be delighted to read it.

Meanwhile feel free to check out our other publications by visiting our Amazon authors page.

Thanks a million you for your purchase – it is much appreciated.

http://amazon.com/author/jamesparis

http://amazon.com/author/normanstone

NOTES/MY TO-DO PAGE

NOTES/MY TO-DO PAGE

CPSIA information can be obtained
at www.ICGtesting.com
Printed in the USA
LVOW04s2129230117

521885LV00017B/886/P

9 781497 325821